My First Colors

READY FOR RED

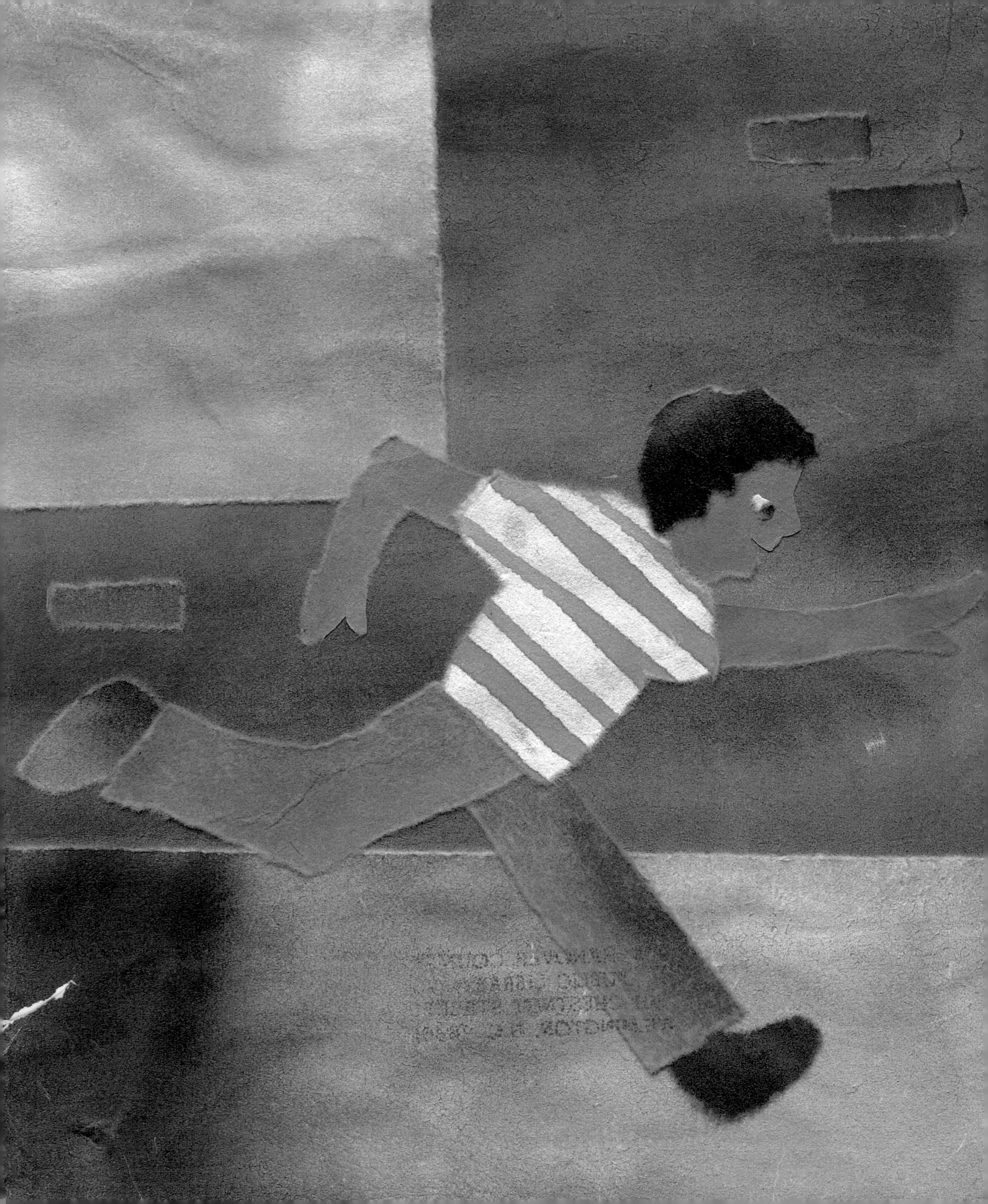

Growing Readers

Purchased with Smart Start Funds

My First Colors

READY FOR RED

by Candace Whitman

ABBEVILLE KIDS
A Division of Abbeville Publishing Group
New York London Paris

Are you ready for red?

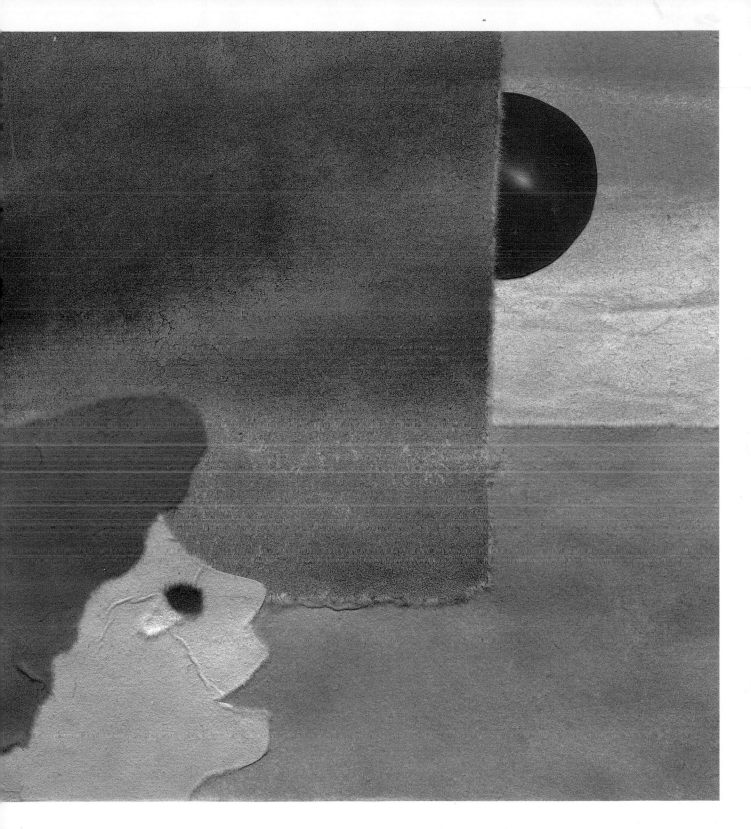

It's just round the corner!

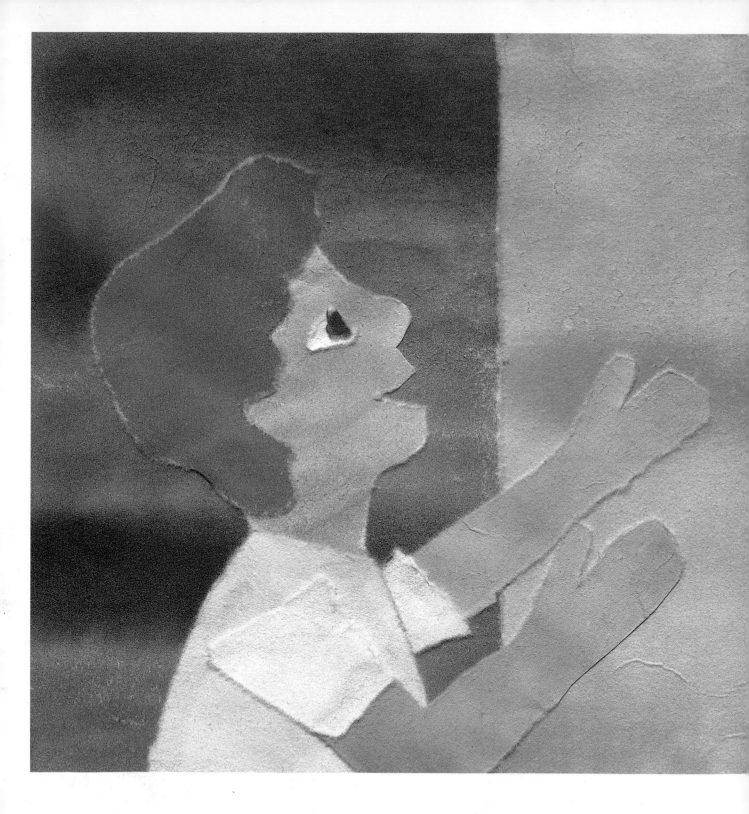

Bouncing to you on a shiny new ball—

Get ready!

See all those roses, ready to bloom?

And the bucket of berries ready for jam?

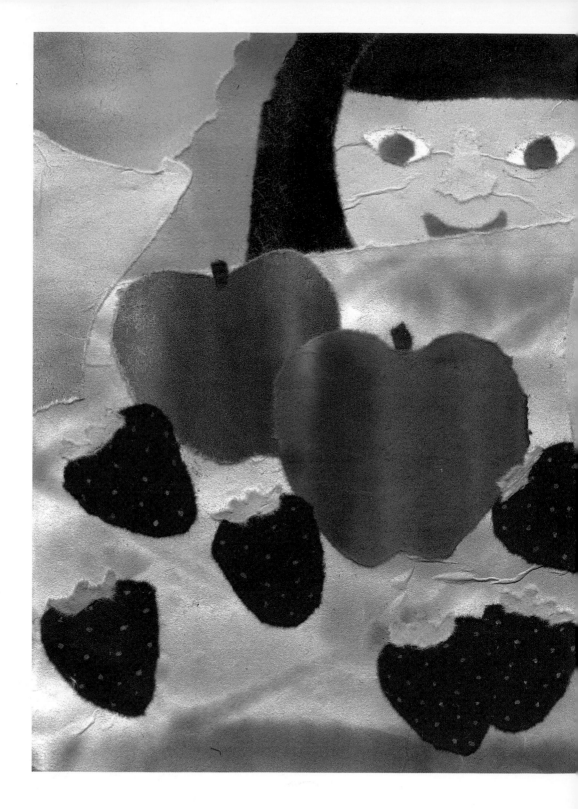

It's time to

make room for red!

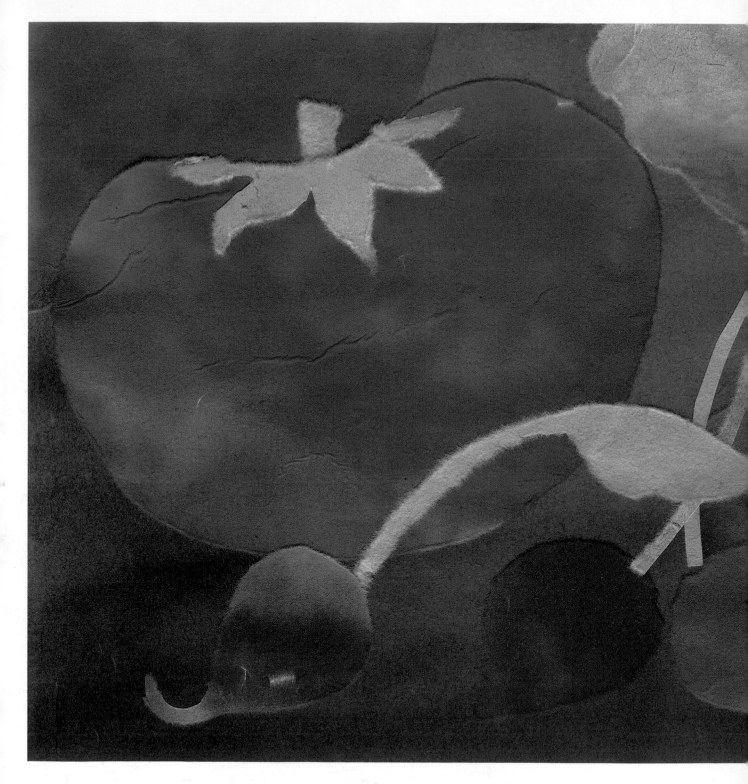

If you're ready for red
You can make quite a salad.

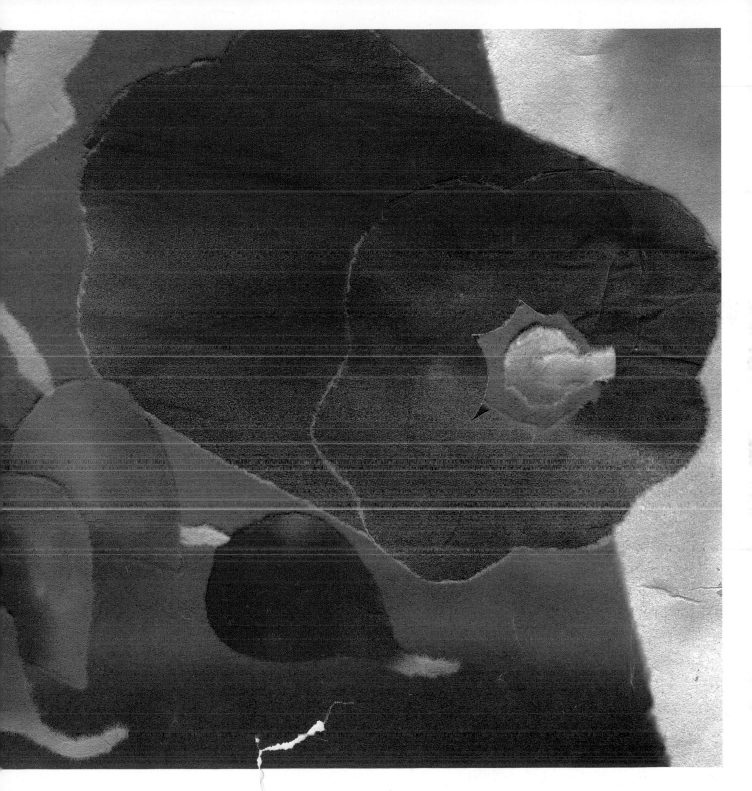

Tomatoes or peppers, which will it be?
Or would a radish or two be better for you?

And back by the barn
Are a rooster and robin
With feathers as bright as their song!

Red
on the corner

The sign says you must stop.
Pausing, waiting, just in time—

A fire truck speeds down the road!

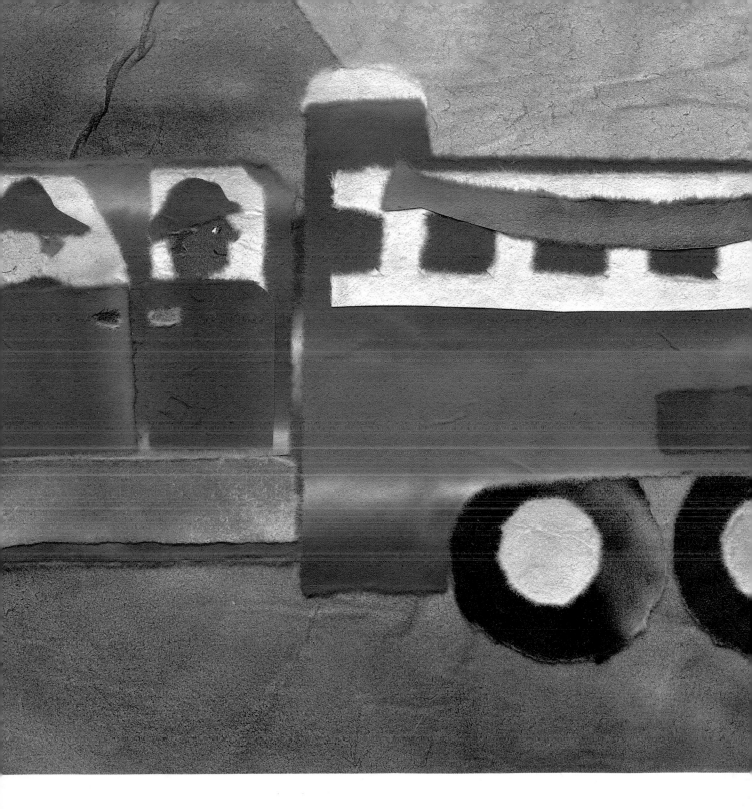

It's red, and it's on to the rescue.

Are you ready for red?
For autumn to end?

Red brightens
autumn's last leaves.

And look! There's red,
coming around

On berries of holly,
And holiday ribbons,

And the cheeks of children

out in the snow.

In winter a fire feels good.
It's red.

Are you ready for red?
Look all around you—

Red is ready for you.

For Jamie

Editors: Leslie Bockol and Meredith Wolf
Designer: Jordana Abrams
Production Manager: Lou Bilka

First edition
2 4 6 8 10 9 7 5 3 1

Library of Congress Cataloging-in-Publication Data
Whitman, Candace, date.
Ready for red / by Candace Whitman. — 1st ed.
p.   cm. — (My first colors)
Summary: Points out how the color red can be found all around us,
in flowers, vegetables, birds, and autumn leaves.
ISBN 0-7892-0311-1
1. Color—Juvenile literature.   2. Red—Juvenile literature.
[1. Red.   2. Color.]   I. Title.   II. Series: Whitman, Candace, date.
My first colors.
QC495.5.W516   1998
535.6—dc21   97-37820